CELTIC TIDE IN CORNWALL

As war
to Cornw
and Brit
and six⌁   ⌁⌁⌁⌁⌁ they
caused a tide to flow which
has affected the lives and
outlook of the people ever since.
 In this brief journey through
the County we visit the sites
of some of these saints. We
also meet others more recently
part of the ebb and flow.
 I hope you will enjoy as much
as I have seeing these places
and getting to know a little
about such remarkable people.

Roger Race

First published 1996 by
M.E. Race and R.E. Sanders : 11, Trennick Row, Truro TR1 1QL (01872 73676)

ST. ANTHONY-IN-MENEAGE

There are not many churches in Cornwall that are named in memory of anyone other than a Celtic saint, but St. Anthony is one.

The name Meneage means "land of monasteries" and there must have been quite a number of them here. This may account for the place being named after St. Anthony, as he was really the founder of this way of life. Originally a monastery merely consisted of a small gathering of like-minded men who shared a life of simplicity and prayer. This is how it would have been at St. Anthony in the early days.

St. Anthony, who was born in 251 AD, was one of the many hermits living in the deserts of Egypt; one of the "Desert Fathers". He was famous for his ability to overcome temptations, and there are many legends of how he dealt with them. His emblem is the pig, and it is said that he made the eating of pork acceptable as it had previously been forbidden by Jewish laws. In the past, monks were given free grazing rights for their herds of swine. Even up to recently the local inhabitants here were called "St. Anthony pigs": Piggy Feast was celebrated on the nearest Sunday to December 26".

We may wonder how this remote spot came to be called St. Anthony. Perhaps the traders from the East, who had been coming to Cornwall for tin for many years, brought the name with them.

Roger Race

BALDHU

This is the church where the vicar was converted in his own pulpit!

The Revd. William Haslam came to this newly-formed parish in 1846, at a time when the area was busy with mining development. Lord Falmouth had bought the patronage and wanted someone to look after the spiritual needs of the three thousand souls in the parish. However, despite the new church and school Haslam was singularly unsuccessful, with few attending church. But things gradually improved and one Sunday it was different. He was preaching his sermon and, he says: "Whether it was something in my words, or my manner or my looks, I know not; but all of a sudden a local preacher, who happened to be in the congregation, stood up and putting up his arms shouted out in Cornish manner:

"The parson is converted! The parson is converted, Hallelujah!" and in another moment his voice was lost in the shouts and praises of three or four hundred of the congregation. Instead of rebuking this extraordinary 'brawling' as I should have done in a former time, I joined in the outburst of praise..... Still the voice of praise went on, and was swelled by numbers of passers-by, who came into the church, greatly surprised to hear and see what was going on."

Haslam's great work here lasted for ten years. Now the church is redundant and deserted, and the parish has been incorporated into the one next door. But the spire still points up to Heaven among the surrounding trees, a reminder of the former glory of the place.

Roger Face

BREAGE

In the churchyard here Lydia Grenfell is buried. She was the young lady Henry Martyn was fond of, but he could not persuade her to go abroad with him.

Henry Martyn, now famous for his translations of the New Testament into Urdu, Arabic and Persian, had met Lydia and a considerable attachment had developed. Emma, Lydia's sister, had told him that his affection was not altogether unreturned. He wrote in his diary: "The discovery gave me both pleasure and pain, but alone at night I resigned myself entirely to the will of God". One day he walked twenty-five miles to see her. He wrote: "The joy of my heart was very great. Every object around me called forth gratitude to God. Perhaps it was joy at the prospect of seeing Lydia — though I asked myself at the time whether, out of love for God, I was willing to turn back, I persuaded myself that I could". Lydia was not at home. He continues: "So I walked out to meet her, and when I met her coming up the hill I was almost induced to believe her more interested in me than I had conceived".

Alas, Lydia could not take the plunge. Whether it was that Henry's love was not sufficiently reciprocated or the fear of travelling to unknown places, we do not know. Poor Henry died of consumption near Constantinople on his way home. It was 1812 and he was thirty-one. Lydia never married and she died at the age of fifty-four after an illness which lasted several years.

ST. CLEMENT

There can be few churches in Cornwall which compare with St. Clement for situation, with its thatched cottages nearby and the Tresillian River at its feet. But who was St. Clement and why was the church named after him?

St. Clement was the third head of the Church after St. Peter, from 91 until 100 AD. He was certainly among the first leaders of the Church before then as he was mentioned in one of St. Paul's letters. Clement is known as the Roman Martyr, his father having been born a Roman. He is especially remembered because of a letter he sent to the Christians in Corinth which helped them to settle a disagreement which had arisen there.

It was due to the circumstances surrounding the death of Clement that the Christian faith spread to the East, to Ukraine and later to Russia. At this time Crimea was a place of exile for those not in favour with the Roman authorities, and this included a large number of Christians. It is tradition that Clement was among those banished here. Evidently his influence was so great that the Emperor, fearing the worst, had him executed. He was bound, tied to an anchor and thrown into the Black Sea. It is because of this that St. Clement is the patron of seafarers and his emblem an anchor.

Was it the remembrance of the martyrdom of St. Clement on similar shores that prompted the seafarers of this place to name their church after him?

ST. ENODOC

The one person who made the visiting of churches a popular pastime was John Betjeman. When he was a child his parents used to bring him to Cornwall on holiday, to their house at Trebetherick beside the Camel estuary. He would cycle down the country lanes, looking for churches. Once he took the ferry to Padstow to explore the other side of the river. He came to St. Ervan and later he wrote about it:

"Dear lanes of Cornwall! With a one-inch map
A bicycle and well-worn 'Little Guide',
Those were the years I used to ride for miles
To far-off churches. One of them that year
So worked on me that, if my life was changed,
I owe it to St. Ervan and his priest
In their small hollow deep in sycamores."

Sir John Betjeman, Poet Laureate and knighted for his contribution to the appreciation of poetry and architecture spent his last days in his "adopted county", as he called it, within sight of the little Norman church of St. Enodoc, the church which a century before had been dug out of the sands which had previously encroached on the site. When he died, his coffin was carried by family and friends across the golf-course, one wet day in May, for him to lie in the small churchyard of St. Enodoc. One of the floral tributes had these words:

"Where train and tram alternate go
The trams have long since gone:
And now we bid a fond farewell
With love to you, Sir John."

Perhaps the best expression of his faith is in this verse of his Christmas poem:

"No love that in a family dwells,
No carolling in frosty air,
Nor all the steeple-shaking bells
Can with this truth compare —
That God was Man in Palestine
And lives today in Bread and Wine."

Roger Race

FALMOUTH

Falmouth is a comparatively modern town, so it is not surprising to find that the parish church here was built as recently as 1662, two years after the Restoration of the monarchy, when Charles II was proclaimed King: and the church was erected with his expressed support. In those days Penryn was the main town and port here: only later did Falmouth become more important.

The church was dedicated to King Charles the Martyr (one of only six in the country to be dedicated to him.) This is evidence of the high regard that was held for him in the County. It had been only sixteen years since the heroic defence of Pendennis Head under the aged Sir John Arundell of Trerice: the Cornish had been very loyal to the King, many

of them having been tenants of Duchy manors. Often in churches in Cornwall there can be seen a painted copy of the Letter of thanks that Charles had sent, acknowledging their support of the Royalist cause.

Not only in Cornwall was the memory of King Charles I revered. In the same year as the church in Falmouth was built the Book of Common Prayer was brought out. It contained a service to commemorate the day of Charles' death – 30th January. This service was taken out of the Prayer Book by order of Parliament in 1859 without the agreement of the Church. But the present Church's Calendar of Festivals and Commemorations includes this date – the day King Charles was martyred.

Roger Race

GUNWALLOE

The little church at Gunwalloe Cove is another instance of one having been founded by a saint from across the English Channel. St. Winwaloe, like St. Melior of Mylor, came from Brittany. He is reputed to have founded the Breton monastery at Landévennac. (Landewednack in Cornwall, a short distance from here, is presumed to have been a small monastery also founded by Winwaloe.) The fact that the part of Brittany where Landévennac is situated is called Cornouaille provides further evidence of this close link in former times.

The beauty of the Cove here is in stark contrast to the desolation of the exposed moors above, particularly Predannack Downs. It was here, after World War 2, that Group Captain Cheshire took over an old disused hut on the edge of a wartime airfield to look after two invalid people and to start the first Cheshire Home.

Later a specially designed Home was built at Long Rock, near Penzance. More were formed elsewhere and now there are over 200 Cheshire Homes spread across 40 countries and caring for more than 4000 people. And it all began in an old hut on Predannack Downs by someone who did not know what to do with himself after a brilliant career in the war.

Leonard Cheshire, like St. Winwaloe, came to these shores to help people in need. No doubt Winwaloe would have said, as Cheshire did:

"To accompany a man on the final steps of his life as a companion and a friend, recognising that it is his special hour in which we are privileged to share, is to receive as much as it is to give."

GWITHIAN

About the year 1540 the traveller and writer John Leland came to Cornwall. At this visit he had the opportunity to read the Lives of the Saints of this area, all of which was destroyed at the Reformation. He was able to record the stories and legends, and among these was the account of the life of Gwinear. He was an Irish prince who had renounced the throne at his father's death and instead decided to lead a missionary band to Cornwall. They landed at Hayle about the year 550 AD and made for Gwithian, then called Conerton, a large town under the local lord called Teudar. Here they were attacked by Teudar and many of them were martyred. Among those in the group was Gothian and he was one of them killed. The memory of this saint must have been so treasured that a church was built here in his honour. The remains of this oratory still exist in the field south of Red River. It is contemporary with St. Piran's oratory at Perranzabuloe, sharing with it the honour of being the oldest church buildings remaining in the country. By the thirteenth century this whole area was becoming covered by sand and already a Norman church had been built further south. There is some evidence of a town of considerable size having existed between the two. Leland describes it as "sumtyme a great toun now gone, 2 paroche chirchis yet scene a good deale several one from the other." The old name survives at Connor Downs, inland in the parish.

Just as the waves of the sea flow over the beach and back again, so also the story of Gwithian reflects the rise and fall of a small particle of civilisation. Once only beach and dunes, it developed into a prosperous town and centre. Then the sands returned and covered it, leaving only the present hamlet, with church, farm, public house and a few cottages.

ST. HILARY

At first sight is seems difficult to understand why a church in Cornwall should have as patron a French saint who was Bishop of Poitiers in the 4⁺ century. The clue lies at St. Michael's Mount which was given by William the Conqueror to Robert, Count of Poitiers, who was his half-brother. So for many years the Mount was tenanted by monks from Normandy who were responsible for the care of the people of the surrounding mainland. So when it came to building a church it was natural that they should think of the great saint who had been so important to them at home. St. Hilary was the first native Celt to become an outstanding force in the Christian movement, and he wrote the first book on the concept of the Holy Trinity. The French connection here is also confirmed by the existence of a spire — most of the few Cornish churches with a spire have something to do with France.

In the 1930s the Vicar, the Revd. Bernard Walke, revived many customs from earlier times, including community religious plays performed by members of the parish (broadcast on the "wireless") together with the enrichment of the decorations within the church. Many contributions to the adornment of the interior were made by local artists and craftsmen. Unhappily some people, mostly from away, objected to these, and much had to be removed. Now the beauty has been restored and the church truly appears as what it is meant to be — a sanctuary of God. In the old days the spire was whitewashed as a guide to mariners, visible from both north and south coasts. The beauty here can still act as a guide to God.

ST. IVES

Like most seafaring folk the fishermen of St. Ives were very aware of their need of the Almighty, and so there are churches and chapels at every turn. They knew the dangers of the sea and that their livelihood depended on it.

One of these old sailors was Alfred Wallis, now acknowledged as one of the foremost British Primitive painters of this century. When he left off sailing, at the age of 70, he started painting from memory, on odd scraps of wood and card, scenes of boats and harbours as he had known them. He was lonely, having recently lost his wife, and he painted "for company." On Sundays there was no painting: he read the Bible, which he called his chart to Heaven. He died aged 87 at Madron Workhouse, but his friends gave him a good grave.

Another painter of the same period but completely different in style was William Titcomb, who was born in 1858, three years after Alfred Wallis. His paintings sold well at the Royal Academy in London. He liked to paint ordinary working people — he was impressed by the simple devotion he often found in them. He liked subjects such as "Piloting Her Home", a death-bed scene, and "Primitive Methodists at Prayer", from Fore Street Chapel. It was in this Chapel that he experienced the great fervour of the worshippers, as when during a service someone called out in a loud voice: "Come down through the roof Lord, and we'll pay expenses." Immediately a large piece of the ceiling fell to the floor!

ST. JUST-IN-ROSELAND

The situation of the church here is typical of an early settlement: a sheltered landing place, isolated and well concealed from marauding pirates. It is named after St. Justus, reputedly the son of King Geraint whose castle was at neighbouring Gerrans. Geraint is said to have been the cousin of King Arthur.

It is the safe anchorage here that gives rise to the legend that Jesus came to Cornwall. It is known that the Phoenicians traded with the Cornish for tin and the legend says that Joseph of Arimathea, who according to the Jewish Talmud was the uncle of Jesus' mother Mary, brought Jesus here as a ship's carpenter. In the Gospels we are told that Joseph was a very rich man, and in St. Jerome's translation of St. Mark's Gospel Joseph is called "Nobilis Decurio", a term denoting an official in charge of metal mines.

Posidonius, the Roman historian, gave details of the tin trading routes :—

across Gaul to Brittany and thence by sea to Britain, to an island called Ictis. Some people think this was St. Michael's Mount, but this is unlikely as the Mount was probably then joined to the mainland. Others say that Ictis is the peninsula of Place and St. Anthony-in-Roseland, and that this was once an island, with the sea connecting Percuil River with Porth Beach at Froe. This means that trading boats could well have come in at St. Just.

It is said that the old people in this area used to talk of the Holy Legend. An old Cornish song had the words: "Joseph was a tin man."

William Blake, the visionary poet, had these thoughts in mind when he wrote his famous "Jerusalem":

"And did those feet in ancient time
Walk upon England's mountains green?
And was the holy Lamb of God
On England's pastures seen?"

LANSALLOS

As in most parishes in Cornwall very little is known about the patron saint, in this case St. Ildierna. William of Worcester, in his visit to the County in the 15ᵗʰ century, was told that the remains of the Bishop St. Hyldren were enshrined in the church, but they were never found. Ildierna, like all the missionaries from Ireland, Wales and Brittany, was venerated as a holy person, but was not a canonised saint of the Church. He or she (it is not certain which) would have originally lived in a hut or cell next to one of the pagan burial grounds which were soon to be adapted for Christian use.

The meaning of the Celtic word "lan" is "a clearing" or "a flat level space," sometimes also understood as "enclosure." It was only later that a monastery would have developed, consisting of a small gathering of wooden huts to accommodate the saint and his or her followers, living an abstemious life-style. At the death of the saint the body was buried in a stone-lined tomb, usually within the "lan." The saint's followers considered it desirable for them to be buried nearby in order to ensure their resurrection, and to be included in the prayers of later pilgrims.

It is likely that there has been Christian worship here at Lansallos for over 1300 years, but if a claim that there was a church here in 284 AD is correct, this would be that much greater.

Roger Race

LELANT

It is possible that Lelant is one of the first places where the Christian faith has been recorded as existing in the British Isles. It is generally accepted that missionaries from Ireland were the first to bring the faith to Cornwall in a big way, but it is possible that there were Christians living here before they arrived. After the year 313 AD there was no prohibition of public worship throughout the Roman Empire and it is now considered likely that there existed small groups of Christian worshippers throughout Roman Britain. There is a Christian memorial stone in Hayle which has been dated at between 350 and 450 AD. This was found at Carnsew, beside the Hayle River estuary, a strategically situated location, which still has evidence of a small earthwork. Part of the story of the Irish missionaries Gwinear (also called Fingar) and Piala tells how when they landed they found a cell inhabited by a holy virgin. At a rock known as Chapel Anja the tiny chapel of St. Anta existed up until the Middle Ages. Lelant was called Lanant (Lan = sacred enclosure, ant = of Anta) as late as 1800.

With the traditions of Christ in Cornwall, tin traders from the Mediterranean and the evidence there is of St. Anta, who can say how early the Christian faith came to Cornwall or where it first took root?

ST. LEVAN

This parish, almost the most westerly in England, has the ingredients of a typical Cornish settlement: the ancient site approached by paths marked by stone crosses, the remains of Norman masonry in the church walls, the fifteenth century tower and south aisle; also the holy well and site of the hermitage beside the sea, probably where St. Selevan lived. There is too a pagan split-stone in the churchyard, confirming that churches were founded on heathen sites.

The church also has a good example of medieval decoration used to instruct the illiterate parishioners. The local legend tells how St. Selevan served a meal to his sister and her two children. Instead of something tasty they were given two chad fish. In their disgust they choked because of the bones. The moral of the story is not to be greedy; and the two fish can be seen carved on one of the bench ends here.

Another bench has a jester — maybe the lesson here is not to be a fool who laughs at the faith of others. Perhaps the best known bench end in Cornwall is the mermaid at Zennor who captivated Matthew Trewella. No doubt the teaching in this case is not to be bewitched by a beautiful woman!

As with the bench ends, all the other features in the church were used to instruct and edify — wall paintings like St. Christopher at Breage reminding people to seek protection for their journeys, stained glass windows telling stories from the Bible and many other decorations employed to get the message across. So now, five hundred years after they were carved, St. Selevan's two fish, the jester and the mermaid still tell their stories.

Roger Race

ST. MAWGAN-IN-PYDAR

Similar to other Celtic oratories in this part of the County this one was founded by a missionary from Wales — St. Mawgan, sometime during the 6° or 7° century, rather later than those further west. The fact that there is another church of St. Mawgan, situated near the south coast, indicates that the saint, like his contemporaries, was a great traveller, probably on his way to Brittany.

After the Norman conquest the land on which this was situated was granted to a family called Lanherne. In the 13° century an heiress of the Lanhernes married an Arundell, and this became the home of perhaps the greatest of that illustrious family. One of the many Sir John Arundells is recorded as having provided King Henry V with 364 men-at-wars and 770 archers. Later, at the time of the Commonwealth the house fell into disrepair, due to the crippling taxes and fines imposed on Catholics. But by 1794 it was sufficiently habitable for Lord Arundell to be able to offer it to some Carmelite nuns who were fleeing from the French Revolution, and they have occupied the house ever since.

St. Mawgan must be unique in that the old faith has been kept here over a period of fourteen centuries. First there was the little cell of St. Mawgan. Later this grew into a monastery. At the Reformation the Arundells kept the candles burning and maintained their form of worship in the private chapel of Lanherne and this has been continued by the Carmelites up to the present.

MAWNAN

The church here is built on an ancient earthwork, still well preserved, which has commanding views over the Helford estuary – another example of the early saints taking over a site formerly used for other purposes.

Two different kinds of saints are remembered here. Firstly, St. Mawnanus who was a Celtic saint, probably from Wales, living here about the 5th or 6th century: little is known about him. Then there is St. Stephen, the first martyr. Many churches throughout the country are dedicated to him. In the 13th and 14th centuries there was a move to question the value of venerating many of the seemingly obscure saints of former times and to conform more with the Roman Calendar of Saints. Here at Mawnan a compromise was settled on, keeping the old Celtic saint in remembrance, but also adding a more standard figure of sanctity of the medieval world. So here we have the church of St. Mawnan and St. Stephen.

Within the parish are situated the well-known gardens of Glendurgan and Trebah, in sheltered valleys coming up from the Helford River, famous for their spring flowers, Camellias & Rhododendrons. These were the homes of members of the Fox family – Quakers, successful trading merchants and philanthropists. Nearby another branch of the family lived at Penjerrick. This was the home of the sisters Anna Maria and Caroline, founders at a youthful age of Falmouth Polytechnic – the first in the country. Caroline, like most young ladies of that time, kept a journal in which she made a note of all the small events and episodes in her quiet, sheltered life, including her disappointment in love. But her most intimate thoughts were kept hidden until after her death. She wrote: "The first gleam of light ….. dawned on

me one day at (a Quakers') Meeting, when I had been meditating on my state in great depression. I seemed to hear the words articulated in my spirit, 'Live up to the light thou hast, and more will be granted thee.' Then I believed that God speaks to man by His Spirit. I strove to live a more Christian life, in union with what I knew to be right, and looked for brighter days."

MORWENSTOW

Perhaps the best known country parson in Cornish history is Robert Stephen Hawker, who was vicar here for over forty years, from 1834 until his death in 1875. He was a poet: one of his poems Tennyson considered to be better than his own on the same theme. And it was Hawker who wrote:

"And shall Trelawny die?
Here's twenty-thousand Cornishmen
Shall know the reason why."

Hawker was active in alleviating the prevailing poverty in the area, and he made a point of visiting every family in his 7,000 acre parish as often as he could. He was always on the beach at storm times helping to rescue shipwrecked mariners, and he would always make sure that the dead were given a good burial.

Hawker was a colourful character, wearing unusual clothes of bright colours, and he always had something appropriate to say on any subject. He was very conscious of the supernatural, saying he once saw a demon leap from the sea as he was riding by on a rough day. He built himself a wooden hut on the cliff edge made of timbers from wrecked ships. He spent many hours there alone. Hawker was thankful for the local traditions of faith and it is claimed he invented the Harvest Festival service. A friend once said of him:

"He believed that God was continually present with His people and that His presence was revealed in ordinary events in human life.......but unlike most of us Hawker was not ashamed openly and continuously to acknowledge it."

MYLOR

For many centuries there was much sea-faring contact between Brittany, Cornwall, Wales and Ireland, extending to the Eastern Mediterranean on one side and to Iceland on the other. Brittany acquired its name through Britons fleeing and settling there at the time when Cornwall (the only part of the country still inhabited by Britons) was being attacked by barbarian hordes from mainland Europe.

Although most of the missions of the fifth and sixth centuries were from Ireland and Wales, quite a number of the early saints were from across the Channel, particularly those whose settlements were along the south coast. St. Mylor (or Melior) was one of them. His settling at this site is corroborated by the existence of a well in the church-yard. (as we have seen, it was the practice of the Celtic saints to take over the customs of earlier religions such as the worship of water and wells.)

The history of Mylor is naturally bound up with the sea. The graveyard has many sad stories to tell of lives lost at sea. There was once a naval dockyard here. During World War II there were army camps hidden under trees nearby, waiting for the invasion of Europe. Remains of slipways can still be seen on some beaches.

After the war some refugees from Ukraine came and settled here. At first they were accommodated in old army huts in fields above the Pandora Inn. Ironically they may well have been among those who had fled from the terrible oppression of their country by Stalin in the 1930s – the very man our armies were preparing to help in battle. The refugees were so thankful to find this safe haven that they erected a stone cross here, a "symbol of faith in God" as the words of the inscription say. The cross is still there, in the grass verge beside the top road leading to Greatwood.

Roger Rudd

ST. NEOT

The first saint to be venerated here was St. Gueryr, whose holy well is down a lane from the village. There is some uncertainty as to whether St. Neot was also a Celtic monk or the well-known relative of King Alfred. It is in a Life of St. Neot that the story is told of Alfred allowing the cakes to burn. This Neot was born a prince and one of the church windows shows him resigning his crown to his younger brother Ethelbald, as he had decided to become a monk. He spent some time as a Benedictine at Glastonbury Abbey and was later allowed to come to the west to live the life of a hermit. He was respected for his piety and humility and sought for his spiritual counselling. He is unusual in being a Saxon saint in Cornwall.

Many of the events in the life of St. Neot are depicted in the stained glass windows which are considered one of the best remaining sets in the country. Miraculously they survived the Civil War and the Commonwealth. Perhaps through the prayers of St. Neot the Cromwellians never came here. In thanksgiving the bough of an oak tree is raised to the roof of the tower each year and secured there for the rest of the year. This takes place on May 29ᵗʰ, Oak Apple Day, the day when Chelsea Pensioners pay tribute to their founder King Charles II, recalling his escape by hiding in an oak tree following the Battle of Worcester — a constant reminder of the allegiance of St. Neot people to the Royal cause.

PERRANUTHNOE

St. Piran, the most popular of the Cornish saints, came to Cornwall in 490 AD. Like most of the saints in the County at that time he had come from Wales, although originally from Ireland; and he was probably on his way to Brittany. He founded his first church at Perranzabuloe, near Perranporth. The remains, now covered by sand, are of one of the oldest Christian sanctuaries in the land. There was continual encroachment of the site by sand driven by the north-westerly gales, and in the 11th century it was abandoned. A new church was built at the end of the parish furthest from the sea.

St. Piran also established a church here at Perranuthnoe. It is probable that this was at a spot now a mile out to sea, having been covered by the rising waters. (It is estimated that the sea has been rising by about nine inches every century.) The present church is comparatively recent, but the founding of the original church by St. Piran is confirmed by the ancient practice of only dedicating a church to a saint if there has already been one in the parish.

St. Piran became the patron saint of tinners, due to the legend that he introduced smelting, having seen a thin stream of the white metal trickling over his hearth. The Cornish flag, known as St. Piran's Cross, with a white cross on a black ground, representing the tin metal among the ore, is said to symbolise the Gospel shining over falsehood.

PHILLACK

Phillack is named after St. Piala, one of the group of missionaries who came from Ireland about 550 AD, landing by the Hayle River. According to a medieval historian named Anselm, Piala was the sister of Gwineor (also called Fingar) who, as we have seen, led the group. Gwinear had renounced the throne and he wanted Piala to marry the new monarch appointed in his place. She declined, saying that Christ alone should be her spouse. She then prepared to accompany him on the journey. On arrival most of the party were martyred by Teudar, the local lord. It is not certain whether Piala was one of those killed, but among those who escaped were St. Ia (St. Ives), St. Meriadoc (Camborne), and St. Uny (Lelant). It is possible that Teudar was a Christian who mistakenly thought he was defending his territory from a raid by the Irish, a common enough event in those days. However, according to the old drama "The Life of Meriasek", which tells the story of St. Meriadoc and is the only medieval miracle play in the Cornish language to survive, King Teudar was himself either beaten or killed by the Duke of Cornwall.

It is part of the tradition that Teudar had his stronghold at Riviere, where the Phillack Youth Hostel is now, just below the church. In the end it was the name of little-known Piala, rather than the great warlord Teudar, that was to be remembered here.

PHILLEIGH

Why is the ferry here called King Harry, and which King Harry or Henry was it?

The simple answer is that a charter for the ferry was granted by King Henry VI. There is a field immediately above the woods beside the ferry on the Roseland side where there are the remains of a chapel which was licensed in 1384 in honour of St. Mary. It was called the chapel of "Our Lady and King Henry" in a document of 1528 in which the proposals for the canonisation of the King were being put forward. All further progress with this cause was prevented by the Reformation, but even today there are many people who feel that he should be honoured as a saint.

It was during the reign of this Henry that England lost most of the land in France that had been acquired by his father. This was through no fault of his, although he got most of the blame for it. It is said that he would have made an excellent priest, being very devout and humble. He dressed simply, often wearing a hair shirt. He was generous to the poor, sometimes sparing the lives of criminals. Once, during one of his imprisonments in the War of the Roses he was struck by a man but he forgave him, saying: "Forsooth, you do foully to smite an anointed King so."

Henry VI is remembered for his founding Eton College and King's College, Cambridge. About being a king he wrote:

"Kingdoms are but cares,
State is devoid of stay:
Riches are ready snares
And hasten to decay."

Roger Race

TREVALGA

Can you imagine a more romantic beginning of a story than that of a young architect arriving to inspect a church in need of repair being met at the vicarage by the beautiful sister-in-law of the vicar? That is what happened to Thomas Hardy. Before starting his writing career he worked for an architect in Dorset, his home county. He had been sent to St. Juliot in north Cornwall to measure up for restoration work to the church. This was in 1872. The young lady, Emma Gifford, evidently took part in the local activities, including conducting the music in church. When the restoration work started Emma laid the foundation stone. The two became very friendly and two years later they were married. They would have seen this view of Trevalga, a neighbouring coastal parish, during their long walks and rides together. (Emma was very keen on horses.)

Hardy's experiences in this beautiful place inspired him to write many of his best poems and later he wrote the partly autobiographical novel: "A Pair of Blue Eyes," drawing on his memories of those happy days. His descriptions of village life of this period are unsurpassed, and we can imagine him sitting in church, looking around and seeing subjects suitable for the characters in his stories. Unfortunately Hardy's own story, like most of his novels, did not have a particularly happy ending, but that is too long a tale to tell now as is so much else we would like to say about this brief journey through Cornwall.

Roger Rac

Acknowledgements are gratefully made to John Murray (Publishers) Ltd. for permission to include excerpts from John Betjeman's "Summoned by Bells" and "Collected Poems", and to Cornwall Historic Churches Trust and Cornwall Tourist Board for their help and encouragement.

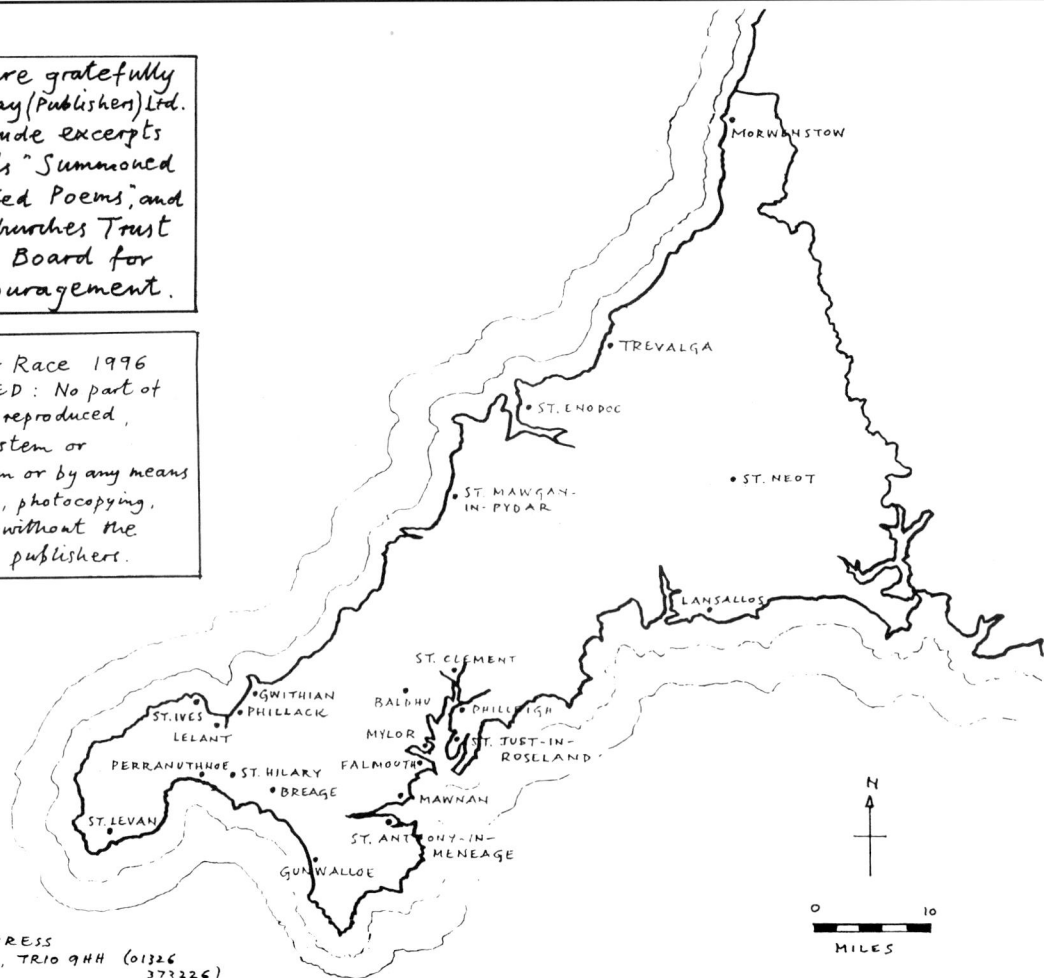

MORWENSTOW

TREVALGA

ST. ENODOC

ST. NEOT

ST. MAWGAN-
IN-PYDAR

LANSALLOS

ST. CLEMENT

GWITHIAN
PHILLACK

BALDHU

PHILLEIGH

ST. IVES
LELANT

MYLOR

ST. JUST-IN-
ROSELLAND

PERRANUTHNOE
ST. HILARY

FALMOUTH

BREAGE

MAWNAN

ST. LEVAN

ST. ANTHONY-IN-
MENEAGE

GUNWALLOE

N

0   10
MILES

PRINTED BY TROUTBECK PRESS
ANTRON HILL, MABE, PENRYN, TR10 9HH (01326
                                         373226)